**This book
belongs to:**

_____

How Jackrabbit
Got His Very
Long Ears

▼ ▼ ▼

How Jackrabbit Got His Very Long Ears

▼ ▼ ▼

BY

Heather Irbinskas

ILLUSTRATED BY

Kenneth J. Spengler

rising moon

Books for Young Readers from Northland Publishing

FIRST EDITION, MAY 1994
Fourth Printing, March 1999
ISBN 0-87358-566-6
Library of Congress Catalog Card Number 93-38250

Library of Congress Cataloging-in-Publication Data
Irbinskas, Heather, 1955-
How Jackrabbit got his very long ears / by Heather Irbinskas ;
illustrated by Kenneth J. Spengler. — 1st ed.
p. cm.
Summary: Because he doesn't listen carefully to what the Great Spirit tells him about each
of the animals he is supposed to lead to their desert homes, Jackrabbit causes much
unhappiness with his careless answers to the animals' questions.
[1. Jackrabbits—Fiction. 2. Desert animals—Fiction. 3. Self-acceptance—Fiction.
4. Behavior—Fiction.] I. Spengler, Kenneth, ill. II. Title.
PZ7.I627Ho 1994
[E]—dc20
93 38250

Designed by Rudy J. Ramos
Edited by Kathryn Wilder Ellis

Manufactured in Hong Kong by South Sea International Press Ltd.

0774/4M/3-99

To my husband, Jonas, who is very special indeed!
—H.I.

To my wife, Margaret, and my son, Matthew,
and to my parents, Ernest and Dorothy Spengler.
—K.J.S.

In the beginning, the Great Spirit made the world. He made the oceans, the mountains, the lowlands, and the forests. Then he mixed a bit of red clay with sand and blew it in each of the four directions, and the great desert of the Southwest was formed. With dabs of paint here and there for yellow and purple flowers, and grays and greens for cactus and desert trees, it was a very pretty picture indeed.

▼   ▼   ▼

Next, the Great Spirit needed a helper to run his errands on earth. After all, a desert isn't made in a day, and the Great Spirit wanted it just so for all the creatures he would put to live there one day. He needed an animal who was fast and smart and would be able to help settle the other creatures into their new desert homes. So, he created Jackrabbit.

▼   ▼   ▼

As the Great Spirit worked to make each animal, he took great time and care, for beneath its beauty the desert hid many dangers for the unwary.   There were thorns on most of the plants. There was very little water, and almost every day the sun burned hot. For outsiders it was quite a forbidding place, but for the desert creatures it would be paradise.

Jackrabbit's job was to take the animals the Great Spirit created and lead them to their new homes. On the way he was to explain, as the Great Spirit had explained to him, just how special they had been made so that they could survive in the desert.

However, there were times when Jackrabbit got bored, and he daydreamed about the days ahead when his job would be done and he and the other animals could gather and play. Because of this, he did not always listen carefully to what the Great Spirit told him about these creatures who were to be his friends.

▼   ▼   ▼

As Jackrabbit took the desert tortoise down to earth, Tortoise asked, "Jackrabbit, why is it that I am so slow?"

Jackrabbit thought a minute, trying to remember what the Great Spirit had said. "Ah, yes," he replied. "It is because you are not as smart as I."

"Oh," said Tortoise, and he sadly walked away.

▼   ▼   ▼

When Jackrabbit took Bobcat down to earth, Bobcat asked, "Jackrabbit, why don't I have a long, beautiful tail instead of this stump?"

Jackrabbit thought a minute, trying to remember what the Great Spirit had told him. "Ah, yes," he replied. "It is because that was all there was—there were no more long tails left."

"Oh," said Bobcat, and he sadly padded away.

▼   ▼   ▼

Then, as Jackrabbit brought Roadrunner
down to earth, Roadrunner asked, "Jackrabbit, why don't I have the wings of an
eagle so that I can soar high in the sky?
I'm only able to fly from the ground to
a tree."

Jackrabbit thought a while, trying to
remember the Great Spirit's words. "Ah,
yes," he replied. "Because you're not as
important as Eagle, so you can't fly as
high as he."

"Oh," said Roadrunner, and she sadly
fluttered away.

When the Great Spirit had finished creating his animals, he looked down upon the desert to see how he had done. The animals had gathered to celebrate their new home. There was lots of laughing and hopping and flying and jumping and general merry-making. The Great Spirit smiled at what he saw, but then he noticed three little figures off to the side. Tortoise, Bobcat, and Road-runner looked very sad indeed.

The Great Spirit came close to them and asked, "How is it that you are so unhappy, my little friends? Don't you like your new home?"

▼   ▼   ▼

Each one nodded, but Tortoise replied with a tear in his eye, "I asked Jackrabbit why it was that you made me so slow, and he said it was because I am not as smart as he."

The Great Spirit said, "Jackrabbit must not have heard me well, because you are special. You alone do not need to run quickly for shelter, because wherever you go you are always home."

"Oh!" said Tortoise, with a smile on his face.

"Jackrabbit said that I have a stump of a tail because you were out of long, beautiful ones," sniffed Bobcat.

The Great Spirit sighed and said, "Jackrabbit must not have listened well, because you, too, are special. A long tail would only have gotten caught on all the thorns and kept you from moving quickly on your way."

"Oh!" said Bobcat, with a twinkle in his eye and a twitch of his short tail.

▼   ▼   ▼

With her head held low, Roadrunner sighed, "I am not important like the eagle in the sky, and that is why I shall never fly as high. That is what Jackrabbit said."

The Great Spirit frowned and said, "Jackrabbit surely did not pay attention, for you are truly special. All that you need is close to the ground, and no one can travel as fast as you across it."

"Oh!" said Roadrunner, and she fluffed her feathers and flexed her toes proudly.

▼   ▼   ▼

As Roadrunner, Tortoise, and Bobcat joined the others, the Great Spirit was thoughtful. "Hmm. Perhaps I made Jackrabbit too quickly," he said to himself. "Not only did he create misunderstandings with his fellow creatures by not paying attention, but a rabbit who does not listen to what goes on around him will not survive in the desert."

▼   ▼   ▼

So that night while the animals slept, the Great Spirit changed Jackrabbit's ordinary rabbit ears to much longer ones—and to this day, if you try to sneak up on a jackrabbit, you'll find he has very good hearing indeed!

Sara Light-Waller

HEATHER IRBINSKAS lives with her husband, Jonas, on a horse farm in Tucson, Arizona, where she trains horses and teaches dressage. Although she has recently become a writer, she has long been a storyteller, illustrating instructions to her riding students with creative tales. A native of Tucson, she demonstrates her compassion for desert creatures in *How Jackrabbit Got His Very Long Ears,* her first children's book. She has also written a film script entitled *The Last Horse Soldier* for Turner Network Television.

Susan Kennedi

KENNETH J. SPENGLER was born in New York City and raised in the suburbs of Philadelphia. He now lives in Sacramento, California, with his wife, Margaret, and son, Matthew. His career as illustrator began shortly after he graduated from Tyler School of Art (Temple University's art school) with a BFA, and his work can be found on anything from posters to billboards, from mystery covers to children's books such as *How Jackrabbit Got His Very Long Ears.*